Woolly Mammoth

by Julie Murray

Abdo
ICE AGE ANIMALS
Kids

Abdo Kids Jumbo is an Imprint of Abdo Kids
abdobooks.com

abdobooks.com

Published by Abdo Kids, a division of ABDO, P.O. Box 398166, Minneapolis, Minnesota 55439.

Printed in the United States of America, North Mankato, Minnesota.

052023

092023

THIS BOOK CONTAINS
RECYCLED MATERIALS

Photo Credits: 123RF, Alamy, Science Source, Shutterstock,
©Jonathan Chen p.1 / CC BY SA 4.0, ©Steve Jurvetson p.7 / CC BY 2.0

Production Contributors: Teddy Borth, Jennie Forsberg, Grace Hansen
Design Contributors: Candice Keimig, Pakou Moua

Library of Congress Control Number: 2022946796

Publisher's Cataloging-in-Publication Data

Names: Murray, Julie, author.

Title: Woolly mammoth / by Julie Murray

Description: Minneapolis, Minnesota : Abdo Kids, 2024 | Series: Ice age animals | Includes online resources and index.

Identifiers: ISBN 9781098266370 (lib. bdg.) | ISBN 9781098267070 (ebook) | ISBN 9781098267421 (Read-to-me ebook)

Subjects: LCSH: Animals--Juvenile literature. | Extinct animals--Juvenile literature. | Ice Age--Juvenile literature. | Paleontology--Juvenile literature. | Zoology--Juvenile literature.

Classification: DDC 569--dc23

Table of Contents

Ice Age

An ice age is a period when most of the Earth is covered by sheets of ice. The last ice age began about 100,000 years ago. It lasted until about 12,000 years ago. Some animals became **extinct** during this time in history.

ice
land

Woolly Mammoth

The woolly mammoth appeared about 300,000 years ago. It lived in Europe, North America, and northern Asia. It was found on grass **steppes**. It is a relative of the elephant.

North America
Europe
Asia
Africa
South America
Australia

The woolly mammoth was a giant animal! It could grow 12 feet (3.7 m) tall. It could weigh up to 16,000 pounds (7,257 kg). Males were bigger than females.

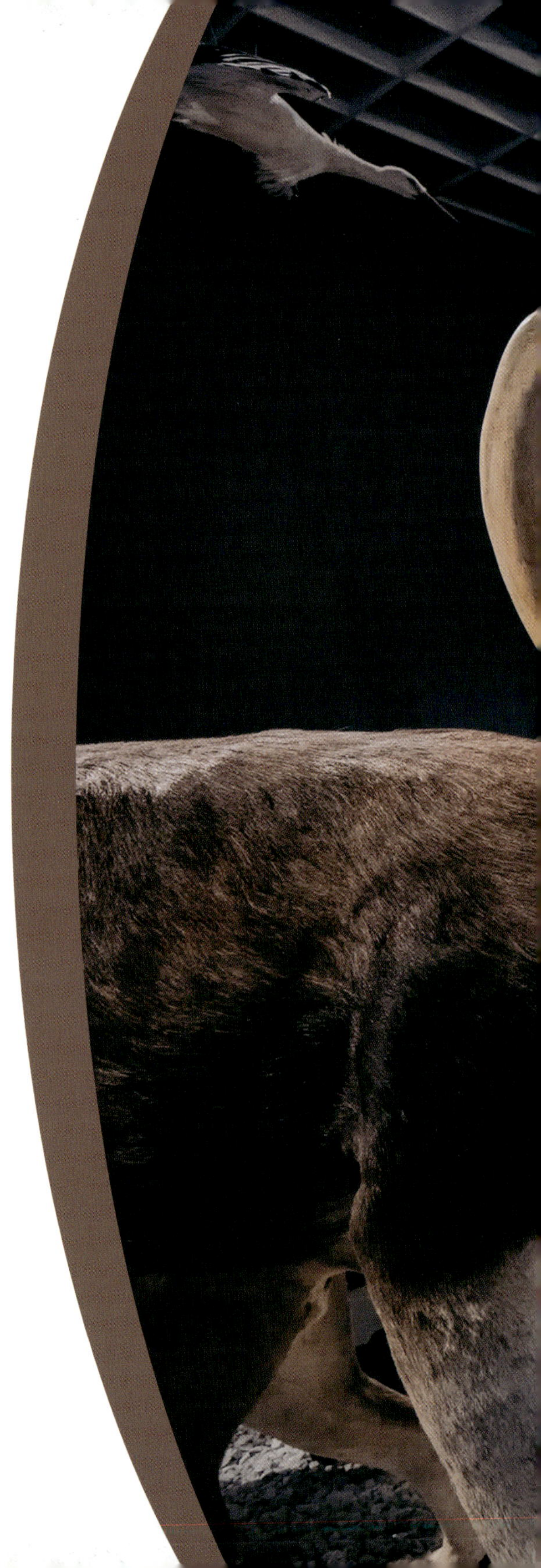

It had small ears and a short tail. Its body was covered in long, shaggy brown hair that kept it warm. Its hair could grow 3 feet (0.9 m) long!

The woolly mammoth had two large teeth called tusks. The tusks could grow up to 14 feet (4.3 m) long. They were used to dig for food and for defense.

The woolly mammoth also had a long, **flexible** trunk. Like modern elephants, it used its trunk to eat and drink.

Food

The woolly mammoth was a **grazer**. It ate grasses and leaves. It could eat up to 400 pounds (181 kg) of food each day!

Extinction

The woolly mammoth became **extinct** about 10,000 years ago. **Climate change** was one major reason for this. Humans were another reason.

Humans hunted the woolly mammoth. They ate its meat. They used its hair to make warm clothes. The tusks and bones were used to make tools and weapons.

More Facts

- The woolly mammoth had giant **molars**. Its molars were used for grinding up food.
- It had a hump on its back that stored fat. This allowed it to survive when food was not easily found.
- It lived in **herds** made up of about 15 woolly mammoths.
- A newborn woolly mammoth was called a calf. It weighed 200 pounds (90.7 kg) at birth!

Glossary

climate change – a change in global and regional climate patterns.

extinct – no longer existing.

flexible – easily bent without breaking.

grazer – an animal that feeds on growing grasses.

herd – a group of animals that feed and travel together.

molar – a large tooth located in the back of the mouth, with a wide biting surface used for grinding food.

steppe – a dry, grassy plain occurring in temperate climates which lie between the tropics and polar regions.

Index